ALL
ABOUT
RABBITS
AS
PETS

Written by KAY COOPER

Photographs by ALVIN E. STAFFAN

JULIAN MESSNER NEW YORK

c1974 64p. il.

ALL
ABOUT
RABBITS
AS
PETS

Published by Julian Messner, a Division of Simon & Schuster, Inc.
1 West 39 Street, New York, N.Y. 10018. All rights reserved.

Text Copyright © 1974 by Kay Cooper Watt
Photographs and drawings Copyright © 1974 by Alvin E. Staffan

Printed in the United States of America
Design by Marjorie Zaum

Library of Congress Cataloging in Publication Data

Cooper, Kay.
    All about rabbits as pets.

    SUMARY: An introduction to rabbits emphasizing their
care, raising, and breeding as pets.
    1. Rabbits—Juvenile literature. [1. Rabbits]
I. Staffan, Alvin E., 1924-   illus. II. Title.
SF453.2.C66   636'.93'22   74-7592
ISBN 0-671-32693-7
ISBN 0-671-32674-0 (lib. bdg.)

For Johno and Jeanne

ACKNOWLEDGMENT

The author acknowledges the kind assistance of Gaston E. McCallister, owner of a rabbitry and member of numerous rabbit breeders associations, and Irving C. Morgan, O.D., both of Springfield, Illinois.

Books by Kay Cooper and Alvin E. Staffan
ALL ABOUT RABBITS AS PETS
A CHIPMUNK'S INSIDE-OUTSIDE WORLD

Contents

Looking at a Rabbit

Hares, cottontails, jack rabbits, and bunnies—these are all names people give to rabbits. But not all of them are rabbits. For example, a hare is not a rabbit at all. It is a different animal. A bunny can be a hare or a rabbit. A jack rabbit is a hare—not a rabbit. And a cottontail is a type of rabbit that has a small white tail that looks like a cotton ball.

The rabbit's ears

The long ears are usually the first thing people notice about rabbits. Swiveling back and forth, the ears pick up the slightest sound from the air.

When a rabbit puts his head down to eat, he keeps his ears straight up, tuned in to his surroundings. Even when asleep, the rabbit twitches his ears and listens.

The rabbit's legs and feet

Nature has also given the rabbit long, powerful hind legs. When the rabbit is alarmed, he strikes the ground with his hind feet, and a loud thumping sound vibrates through the earth. The sound is felt and heard by other rabbits nearby and serves as a warning for them.

To escape danger, the rabbit leaps into the air, and in

◄ Rabbits keep their ears up, even while eating.

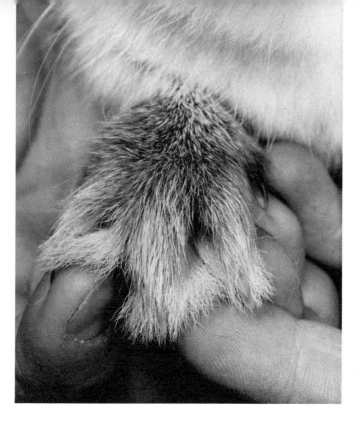

The padded thick fur of
the rabbit's foot. Front foot
(upper). Hind foot (lower).

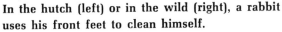
In the hutch (left) or in the wild (right), a rabbit uses his front feet to clean himself.

a few long jumps he can cover fifteen feet. His hops become shorter and shorter until finally he plunges into some bushes. He doesn't move. He sits like a dark rock in the undergrowth until the danger passes.

As soon as it is safe, the rabbit moves away. Now he hops along slowly, covering only a few inches at a time. In between hops, he sits up and looks around.

The rabbit's feet, padded with thick fur, give him a firm hold on rocks and in slippery snow. Each hind foot has four clawed toes, while each front foot has five clawed toes.

To clean himself, the rabbit uses his front feet as if they were hands. Moistening his paws with the saliva on his tongue, he rubs his feet all over his face. He licks the other parts of his body.

// 11

A rabbit likes to dig. With his front paws he loosens the earth, while his hind feet kick the dirt behind him. Some rabbits build long burrow homes; others dig a small hole for a nest in which their babies are born.

The rabbit's tail

The rabbit has a short, furry tail that is turned up at the end. Sometimes the underside of the tail is white and resembles a cotton ball. Rabbits with tails like this are called "cottontails."

When the rabbit is excited, he flashes his tail up and down. He turns it up when running.

A cottontail's tail looks like a cotton ball.

The rabbit's eyes

The rabbit's eyes are located on the sides of his head, not in front like those of human beings. Because of this, the rabbit can see almost all the way around himself without turning his head. He has only one blind spot. It is directly behind his head.

The location of the rabbit's eyes affects the way that he sees things. A rabbit uses both eyes to see something directly in front of him. When he does, he sees the way we do. He can see depths, and he can judge distance. But if he is looking at something on either side, his eyes are too far apart to work together. His right eye sees only

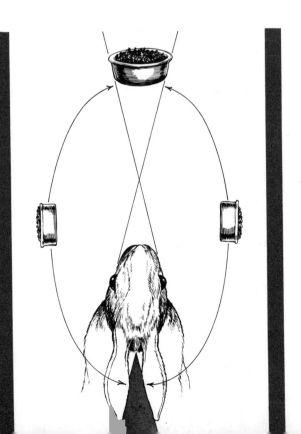

The location of the rabbit's eyes affects the way he sees things.

These teeth grow continuously and are worn down by the rabbit's gnawing.

things on his right side. His left eye can see only things on the left side. He cannot judge distance or depths, and objects appear flat.

A rabbit cannot see color. He sees things only in shades of gray. This is because rabbits lack structures, called cones, in the retina of the eye that are sensitive to colors.

The rabbit's teeth

When a rabbit eats, he first nibbles. Then he settles back, lifts his head, and, with a sideways motion of his jaws, slowly munches his food.

Most rabbits have 28 teeth. The most interesting are the long cutting teeth, or incisors. Two pairs of incisors are located in the upper front part of the rabbit's mouth, one pair directly behind the other. Another pair is in the front part of his lower jaw. These teeth continuously grow and are worn down by the rabbit's gnawing on green twigs and bark. All rabbits are plant eaters.

How to tell a rabbit from a hare

Hares are usually larger than rabbits. They generally have longer legs, and their ears, which are tipped black, are longer, too.

However, the real scientific differences between rabbits and hares are in their skulls and in the appearance of their young at birth.

Most rabbits are born naked. Their eyes and ears are closed and usually do not open until they are about seven days old. Baby hares are born with furred coats and open eyes. It takes baby hares a longer time to grow inside their mother's body than it takes baby rabbits.

Rabbits have become confused with hares because some of them have been misnamed. For example, the North American jack rabbit and the snowshoe rabbit are not rabbits. They are hares. The swamp hare and Belgian hare are not hares. They are rabbits.

What's a bunny?

The word "bunny" comes from the Old French word

bugne, meaning a soft, watery swelling on the joints of animals. From this meaning came the expression "soft as a bunny." Since a rabbit's fur is soft, he too came to be called a bunny. Now many people simply call all rabbits and hares bunnies.

The most popular bunny of all is the Easter Bunny. Legend says that he hides decorated eggs in houses and yards every year at Easter time.

No one knows why there is an Easter Bunny or why he hides eggs. According to one story, the ancient people of England and Europe believed their spring goddess, Ostara (or Eostre), changed a bird into a rabbit. Happy with his new shape, the rabbit laid eggs for Ostara in the spring of the year. Later, when these people became Christians, they celebrated Easter, which occurred around the same time as the old springtime celebration. This egg-laying rabbit then became the Easter Bunny.

The Rabbit's Scientific Name

There are so many different kinds of animals on earth that scientists have named and classified them all into a system.

All animals belong to the animal kingdom, which is divided into phyla. Each phylum (the singular of "phyla") is broken down into smaller groups called class, order, family, genus, and species.

It is important to remember this sequence: Kingdom, phylum, class, order, family, genus, and species. An easy way to do this is to think of the sentence "King Philip Can Order Five Great Specimens." The first letter of each word is the same as for each of the seven divisions.

Suppose you want to classify one of the rabbits found in the United States. The Eastern cottontail rabbit, for example, belongs to the kingdom <u>Animalia</u> and the phylum <u>Chordata</u> (animals with a backbone). His class is <u>Mammalia</u> (animals that nurse their young). He belongs to the order <u>Lagomorpha</u>, which means "hare-shaped." His family name is <u>Leporidae</u>, meaning "hare." His genus is <u>Sylvilagus</u>, which means "wood hare." His species name is <u>floridanus</u>, meaning "of Florida."

All words in the classification system are Latin words. Latin is used so that all scientists throughout the world, no matter what their national language is, can understand each other.

The scientific name of each animal consists of the last two divisions in this classification system. The generic, or genus, name is like your family name. The species name is like your first name. So the Eastern cottontail rabbit's scientific name is <u>Sylvilagus floridanus</u>.

Rabbits were once classed as rodents

Rabbits were once classified in the largest order of mammals, <u>Rodentia</u>. This order includes the rodents: mice, rats, guinea pigs, beavers, and porcupines. All these animals // **17** have long incisors like rabbits. And, because rabbits and rodents were alike in this way, they were grouped together.

In recent years, however, scientists have learned that rabbits are not like rodents at all. Even their incisors are different. Rodents have only two pairs of incisors, while rabbits have three.

Wild Rabbits and Where to Find Them

In the fields, deserts, woods, mountains, and swamps of the United States live animals that resemble ancient creatures. They are wild rabbits. These animals do not look too different from the rabbits that lived 40 million years ago.

Unless you live in the middle of a large city, you can see wild rabbits throughout the year. Certain types called cottontails are found in every state. They are easy to identify, for they all have white tails that look like puffs of cotton.

Although there are 13 different kinds of cottontails in North and South America, they all have the same general color. Brown hairs sprinkled with black cover most of their bodies. Their bellies are white, and the tops of their hind feet are usually white or tan. Cottontails weigh from two to six pounds, and grow from ten to 22 inches long.

Like all rabbits, cottontails are shy animals. You may have to sit quietly without moving for a long time until one appears. To be sure you are in an area, where they live, examine plants for gnawing marks made by the rabbit's teeth. Soft bark is food for the rabbit. When the rab-

Look closely and you may see a cottontail.

bit gnaws on small trees and shrubs, his teeth carve upside-down V markings on the bark.

Look for rabbit tracks, too. They will be in the sand, snow, mud, and dust. The rabbit leaves footprints arranged in a pattern that is easy to recognize. When a rabbit hops, he rears up on his hind legs and pushes himself off the ground. He lands by placing his front feet down first, one in front of the other. He kicks his hind feet up into the air and then swings them down, ahead of his front feet. The rabbit is now ready to push off again.

The best time to spot cottontails is in the early morning, late afternoon, or early evening. At these times, the plants are beaded with dew, and provide the cottontail with water as well as nourishment.

The cottontail's home is usually a "form," or sitting place. He makes it by scratching the earth with his front paws until he forms a shallow hole. Here he sits most of the day, resting and cleaning himself. Forms are hard to find because they are well hidden in thick clumps of grass and under piles of brush.

In winter, cottontails may move into the woods, where there are more plants to protect them from the snow and cold winds. They use the deserted dens of woodchucks and skunks for homes.

Rabbit tracks in the snow.

A cottontail
resting
in its form.

If there is a swampy area near your house, look along its shores for the swamp or marsh rabbit. The largest of the cottontails, the swamp rabbit is from 16 to 22 inches long and weighs about six pounds. His legs are covered with short brown hair. The rest of his body has longer, brownish-gray hair.

The swamp rabbit is a good swimmer. His large feet have spread out toes that enable him to swim through the water in a flash. Sometimes, he dives into the water, pops back up to the surface, and hides there with only his nose and ears showing. But most of the time, he likes to sit and rest on stones and logs projecting out of the water.

Another type of wild rabbit is the Old World rabbit. As his name suggests, this rabbit first inhabited the Old World continents of Europe and Africa. Many thousands of years ago in Africa, some of these rabbits were tamed and became used to living with man. It is from these rabbits that all domestic rabbits are descended.

The Old World rabbits were brought to the United States by English immigrants in the mid-nineteenth century. Many of them were taken to several islands off the coasts of Washington, California, and Alaska. There the farmers raised the rabbits for meat. Later, when the farming business failed, the farmers released the rabbits. Any domestic rabbit will become wild if given the chance. And so after a number of generations, the rabbits on the islands were wild.

22 // You can find them in the fields and open woodlands.

They dig burrow homes with many tunnels and chambers in which they live and raise their young. They come out of their burrows in the evening, and return before morning.

Pet Rabbits

Since rabbits were first domesticated, they have made fine pets. They rarely bite, and are very gentle. They are clean animals and are easy to keep. Like cats, rabbits can be housebroken and taught to use litter pans.

Domestic rabbits, however, are the only kind of rabbits that make good pets. Wild rabbits, such as the Eastern cottontail rabbit, should never be kept as pets. Wild rabbits are hard to raise and will bite. If they are kept as pets, they will become very unhappy and often sick. In most states, it is illegal to keep wild rabbits (or any wild animals) as pets.

Once you have a rabbit for a pet, he is your responsibility. Before you bring him home, make sure you will be able to take good care of him. Think about the answers to the following questions.

What are the costs for food, cages, and special equipment, such as bowls and clippers? Will you take the time to clean his cage and feed him? How will your rabbit be cared for when you go on a trip? Rabbits cannot be left alone overnight because they need fresh water and food every day.

Selecting a pet rabbit. Sometimes rabbits' ears are marked for identification. It does not hurt the rabbit and wears off in a few days.

Always stroke your rabbit in the direction in which the fur lies.

It is also a good idea to think about what you can do with your rabbit if you should no longer wish to keep him. Can you sell him as a pet or a breeder, or donate him to a children's zoo or school?

When you are ready to get your rabbit, look for rabbits for sale in the advertisement section of your newspaper under such headings as "Pets," "Livestock," or "Poultry." You can also buy rabbits at some pet stores. Or perhaps someone you know has many rabbits and will give you one.

In some areas, pet rabbits are hard to find. You can get a list of rabbitries (places where rabbits are kept and bred)

Pet rabbits are fun to play with.

by writing to the American Rabbit Breeders Association, P. O. Box 348, Bloomington, Illinois, 61701.

Once you have your rabbit, select a name for him and call him only by that name. In time he will come to you when called. He will like to sit on your lap and be petted. When you stroke him, be sure to move your hand in the direction that the fur lies.

Pet rabbits are fun to play with and watch. They like to play the game "roll the can." Roll an empty soft drink can to your rabbit, and he will roll it back to you with his nose. Your rabbit also will untie your shoelaces with his teeth.   // 25

Choosing your rabbit

Healthy rabbits, of course, make the best pets. You can tell whether a rabbit is in good health if he is alert and hopping around in his cage. His eyes should be bright and clear. His fur will feel soft. His belly should be plump.

Rabbits of either sex are ideal pets. But don't get a male and female if you don't want to raise rabbits. A female (doe) rabbit's cage, however, is easier to keep clean. She does not spray urine around her living quarters as a male (buck) rabbit will do.

To tell the sex of newborn rabbits, turn the rabbit on its back and hold it firmly in one hand. Gently pull back the tail with your other hand and look at the sexual open-

Sexing—young doe (left) and young buck (right).

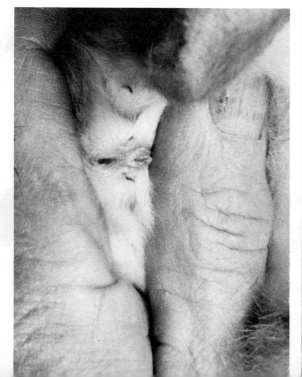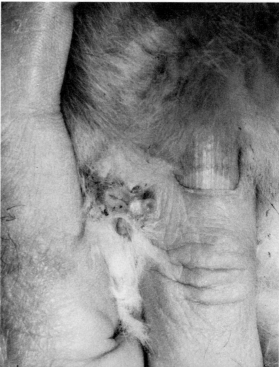

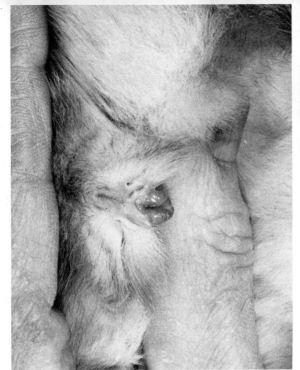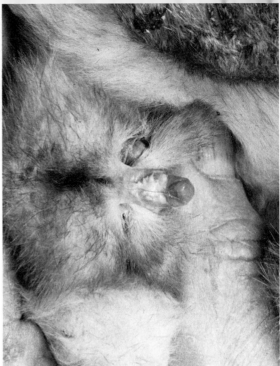

Sexing—adult doe (left) and adult buck (right).

ing, which lies between the hind legs and in front of the anus. (The sexual opening is part of the rabbit's reproductive system, and the anus is the opening through which solid wastes are passed from his body.)

If the anus and sexual opening are close together, then the rabbit is a doe. If the distance is farther apart, then you have a buck. You will have to compare several rabbits before you can tell the difference.

It is easier to tell the sex of month-old rabbits. Press gently on the sides of the sexual opening with your fingers. In bucks, the opening is round. A small penis will appear from the hole. The penis is shaped like a tiny pencil and has an opening in the tip. Through this opening passes urine and sperm, the male sex cells.

In does, the sexual opening is a long slit. The clitoris, which is part of the female's sexual structure, is flat and has no opening in the tip.

How to handle rabbits

The correct way to pick up a rabbit is to grasp the loose skin over his shoulders with one hand. At the same time, slip your other hand under his rump to support his weight. Lift him with one hand; support him with your other hand.

Heavy rabbits may be carried backwards under your arm. Hold the rabbit against your side, and keep his head tucked under your arm. Remember, rabbits are easily frightened. Cover his face with your arm so his eyes are hidden from sights that might alarm him.

Never lift rabbits by their ears or legs. Their delicate ears may break. Quite often, a rabbit lifted by his legs becomes frightened and kicks his hind feet so hard that he breaks his backbone.

Showing your rabbit

Most pet rabbits are purebred. This means that their parents, grandparents, and great-grandparents are all alike in shape and color. These animals, along with others like them, form a breed.

◄ The correct way to pick up a rabbit.

Other pet rabbits are mixed and have parents of different breeds. Both kinds make good pets.

If your rabbit is purebred, his original owner will give you a piece of paper that lists the names of the rabbit's family. This is your rabbit's pedigree or family tree.

You might want to enter your purebred rabbit in rabbit shows. Ribbons are awarded to the best rabbits according to their color, size, and weight. You can get a list of rabbit shows in your area by writing to the American Rabbit Breeders Association.

Even if you have a mixed breed, you can show him —either in shows organized with your friends or classmates or in the 4-H club shows.

All Kinds of Rabbits

Today there are about 50 breeds of domestic rabbits. (See breed list on pages 60-62). They come in a variety of colors and color patterns, many of which are quite spectacular. There are black and white Dutch rabbits, which look like miniature panda bears, and Siamese satin rabbits, which resemble a breed of cat called Siamese.

Some rabbits have fur of many colors. If you look at a Chinchilla rabbit, for instance, you will discover that each hair has at least three colors—dark blue, light pearl **30 //** (dull gray), and black.

**Prize-winning
Chinchilla Satin**

Himalayan

**New Zealand
White**

**Netherland Dwarf,
White**

Dutch, Black

Flemish Giant (largest breed) with Netherland
Dwarf, Black (smallest breed).

Lops

Most rabbits are short-haired. Others, called Angoras, are long-haired. Angoras need extra care because their long wool coats must be combed with a wire brush regularly and checked daily for tangles.

As a rabbit grows, he sheds his fur or molts. New hair grows under the old hair, which slips out of the rabbit's skin and falls off. Sometimes the new hair is a shade darker or lighter than the old hair.

With the exception of the large rabbits (giant Chinchilla, checkered giant, and Flemish Giant), which are too heavy for you to carry properly, all domestic rabbits make good pets whether they are long-haired, short-haired, white, or multicolored.

Angora

Californian

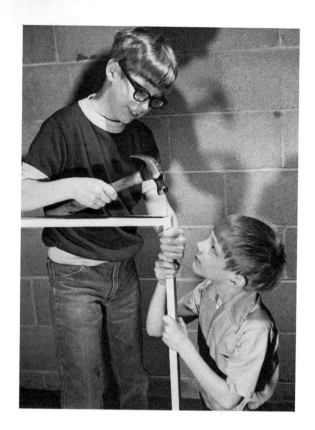

These boys built a simple hutch 3'x2'. They used 1"x2" pine wood fastened with nails and covered with 1" chicken wire.

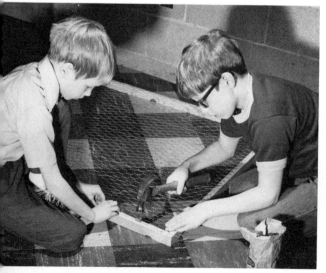

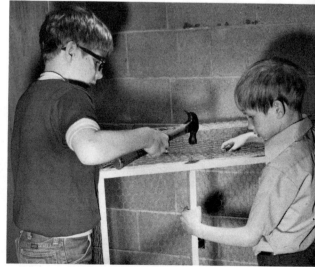

Homes for Rabbits

Rabbits should be kept in special wire cages called hutches. These hutches come in several sizes, and can be purchased at pet shops, rabbitries, or rabbit supply firms, or they can be homemade.

A hutch that is completely made of wire (including the floor) is the best home for a rabbit. It is easy to clean. And it allows fresh air to move around the animal and keep him cool.

If you have this type of hutch and your rabbit weighs nine pounds or more, he will need a bunny board. This is a flat piece of wood on which your rabbit can sit. Such a resting place prevents his feet from becoming sore.

A board about 12 inches wide and 24 inches long makes a good size. Make sure the surface is slightly rough. That way the rabbit's feet will not slip on the board.

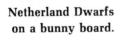

Netherland Dwarfs on a bunny board.

Outdoor living

If you keep your rabbit outside, the best places for the hutch are in a garage, in a barn, on a porch, or under a roof. Make sure the hutch is at least two and a half feet above the ground, in order to protect the rabbits from other animals in your neighborhood.

During the winter, rabbits need some kind of litter or bedding material to keep warm. You can put hay, straw, or dried and broken leaves in the hutch. Don't use sawdust or rags, for if these materials get wet, they will not dry out fast enough and your rabbit could become chilled, get ill, and die. You can also nail pieces of canvas on the sides of the hutch and lower them when the weather is bad.

Be sure to clean the hutch once a week. First, remove the rabbit and place him in a box that is securely fastened. Then spray the hutch with a disinfectant, such as Lysol, to destroy germs.

Before putting your rabbit back, make sure the hutch is completely dry.

Droppings, and soiled hay and straw should be removed daily.

A finished hutch. Food and water are in separate bowls (see page 39); hay covers the floor; and, there is a salt block fastened to the side (see page 42).

Indoor living

In the house you can keep rabbits in a hutch, an orange crate, a large cardboard box, or a large aquarium. The best location for the hutch is next to a window that faces north, or one that is so shaded by outdoor plants that it never receives the direct rays of the sun. Make sure that you use a wire screen, tightly fastened, to cover your rabbit's home. Rabbits are expert jumpers.

In time, rabbits will nibble through a cardboard box or orange crate. However, you can prevent this by nailing wire screening to the interior sides and bottom. Always put the smoother side of the screening inward or upward. A tray, metal sheet, or newspapers should be put on the bottom of the cage. If you use newspapers, replace them every day with fresh ones.

Feeding Rabbits

Feeding rabbits is easy and does not take much time. However, they must be fed at about the same time every day. Rabbits learn to expect food at a certain time and become hungry if they are not fed. This could affect their health.

You can give your rabbit its food all together, once a day, or divide it into two feeding times. If you decide to feed your rabbit once, evening is the best time. This is because rabbits are night feeders. Young rabbits, however, must be fed once in the morning and once at night.

Don't overload your rabbit with food. Rabbits usually keep eating if there is food. As a result, they can become very fat, and fat rabbits tend to get sick easily and will not breed. Overfed does may die having their babies or fail to nurse.

Food and water should be placed in separate containers inside the hutch. Pet shops sell heavy crockery bowls that are ideal for rabbits. These bowls are sturdy and are not easily knocked over by the rabbit. You can also use tin cake pans or small pottery bowls.

Grains

The best food for rabbits are dry rabbit pellets. Pellets contain all the things rabbits need to stay healthy: yellow corn, ground oats, soybean meal, alfalfa, vitamins, minerals, and other substances. Pet shops and feed stores sell various brands of pellets.

Some rabbits like one brand; some like a different kind. Still others like lamb and horse feed. Whichever brand your rabbit likes, continue to use it. Don't switch from brand to brand, as your rabbit may become ill.

A ten-pound rabbit eats about six ounces of pellets a day. A smaller rabbit eats three or four ounces. And a baby rabbit eats two or three ounces. One heaping handful of pellets makes about an ounce.

One heaping handful
of pellets makes
about an ounce.

Within a month, you will know if you are feeding your rabbit the right amount of food. If you can feel his backbone and ribs, he needs more food. If he looks too fat, feed him less.

Rabbits enjoy one raw carrot, a small sweet potato, sugar beet, or turnip once a day. You can also give them lettuce or watercress once a day. However, too many greens may upset your rabbit's stomach.

Never give your rabbit cabbage leaves, greasy foods, or meat. All these foods will make your rabbit sick.

Water

Rabbits need lots of water. During hot weather, one rabbit can drink two quarts a day! In cold weather, they

Rabbits enjoy a raw carrot once a day.

don't need so much. Water bowls should be cleaned once a week by carefully rinsing them with boiling water.

Water kept in an outdoor hutch may freeze in cold weather. To prevent this, fill the bowl with warm water and put it in the hutch just before feeding time. When the rabbit has finished drinking, remove the bowl.

Vitamins

Rabbits get some of their nourishment by passing most of their food twice through their bodies. They have two kinds of droppings—dry ones and soft, moist ones.

After the rabbit eats, the soft droppings are formed inside his body and passed from the anus. Rabbits then eat these soft dropping which go back through the body and are passed out of the anus as dry droppings.

// **41**

The soft droppings the rabbit eats contain protein and certain B vitamins that are thought to be formed by bacteria in the intestines. These substances are used by the rabbit's body when the food goes through the second time.

Salt

Rabbits need extra salt to stay healthy, because there is not enough in their food. You can give them the extra salt in one of two ways. Either sprinkle a little salt on their pellets twice a week, or buy a block of rock salt at a pet shop or feed store.

Salt blocks can be easily fastened to the hutch with a screw. Place the block about six inches above the hutch floor so the rabbit can easily reach it. Your rabbit will lick the salt as he needs it.

Your Rabbit's Health

A rabbit is basically a healthy animal. Like any pet, however, he depends on you to take care of his health.

He needs you to keep his hutch clean, to give him plenty of fresh water, and to feed him every day. He needs sunshine and fresh air. And he must be protected from the rain, direct sunlight, and cold winds.

Like other animals, rabbits can become ill. Sneezing and a running nose are usually signs of a cold or allergy. You can treat your rabbit by keeping him warm and dry. For a running nose, squeeze two drops of regular nose drops into each nostril twice a day. If he doesn't become better in a week, take him to a veterinarian (animal doctor).

A swollen, hard, and hot stomach are signs of pot belly. Your rabbit may breathe in short, shallow breaths, and refuse to eat. Pot belly is caused by inactivity and by eating damp or moldy greens. You can treat your rabbit yourself by feeding him smaller amounts of his pellets, giving him no green foods at all, and letting him run

Nose drops for a cold.

around on the lawn or in the house. If your rabbit is not better within a week, consult a veterinarian.

Sore feet or hocks is another ailment a rabbit can develop. This happens when rabbits live on rough or wet floors, or on damp straw and hay. Their feet will look red and sore. You can treat sore hocks by keeping the pads of the feet and the hutch dry.

Sometimes, a yellowish-white fluid forms in the sores. If this happens, wash the pads with warm water and soap. Dry them thoroughly and rub in an ointment, such as petroleum jelly. (Ask your local pharmacist for petroleum jelly with carbolic acid). Continue this treatment once a day until all the sores have healed.

If you see your rabbit shaking his head and scratching his ears too often, he probably has ear canker. This ailment is caused by mites. These tiny creatures live so deep within a rabbit's ears that you cannot see them. Ask your pharmacist for some sweet oil. Use a cotton ball or swab to smear the oil over the opening of the ear. The oil will work its way into the ear and suffocate the mites.

Raising a Family

If you decide to raise rabbits, you must be sure that you have a doe (female) and a buck (male). You might

44 // want to have both as pets, or perhaps you can mate your

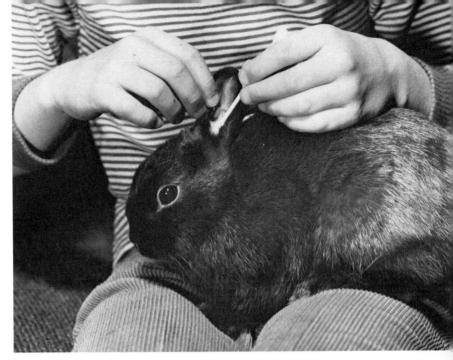

Sweet oil for ear canker.

rabbit with a friend's. Or you might ask around school or in your neighborhood for the rabbit you need.

A doe that is not ready to mate will probably bite the buck. You can tell when she is ready to mate by watching her. She will hop restlessly around her hutch, and rub her chin on her feeding bowls. Now it is time to place her in the buck's hutch. <u>Never</u> put the buck into the doe's hutch. She will attack him.

When rabbits mate, the buck will lift his tail and flash it at the doe. Quickly, he nudges her with his hip and dampens her tail with urine. In response, the doe lowers her back, lifts her head, and flicks her tail.

The male may mount the female several times. His penis enters a narrow passageway in the doe's body called a vagina. Sperm, or male sex cells, pass from his penis and flow into the passage. Swimming up the vagina, the sperm travel through two parts of the doe's body called uteri (plural for uterus) and into the tubes, where egg cells soon will be shed by two glands called ovaries.

After the sperm are released, the buck pulls away from the doe and falls over on his side. He may even squeal. Now copulation (mating) is completed, and you can return the doe to her hutch.

In ten hours, the doe ovulates, or produces eggs

Mating.

within her body. The eggs move through the doe's body and join some of the sperm that came from the buck. The sperm enters the egg, and together they become one new life, which will form into a baby rabbit.

You can tell if your doe is pregnant by a simple test. About ten days after mating, place her in the buck's hutch again. If she growls or tries to escape from him, she is probably pregnant. Once the doe is pregnant, she does not want to be bothered by the buck.

Sometimes, rabbits will not mate the first time. If this happens, return the doe to the buck's hutch in three days. It may take several visits before the doe feels comfortable with the buck. Then they will probably mate.

Nest box

As soon as your doe is pregnant, start getting ready for the birth of the babies. You will need a metal or wooden enclosure for a nest box.

Most rabbitry equipment manufacturers sell nest boxes. The American Rabbit Breeders Association will send you a list of these places. You can also make a nest box with wood and nails. The exact size will vary according to the breed of rabbits you raise.

Fill the nest box with enough clean straw or excelsior so that the doe will have to burrow in it to form her nest. Excelsior (curled shreds of wood) is used for packing furniture and bottles. Drug and furniture stores are good places to find it. Straw and excelsior soak up the young rabbits' urine, and help keep the animals warm.

In summer, the top of the nest box should be open. This allows moisture in the nest to rise and escape, and keeps the rabbits from becoming too hot.

In winter, the top of the nest box should be kept closed. This prevents heat from escaping and keeps the young rabbits warm. For extra warmth in freezing weather, place the nest box inside a large cardboard box.

You can also use an electric nest box warmer instead of a cardboard box to warm the nest box. A warmer can be purchased from equipment manufacturers.

One week after the young rabbits come out of the nest box, remove it from the hutch. Clean and spray the nest box with a disinfectant, and store it in a safe place.

Taking care of the doe

The period of gestation, or pregnancy, is about 31 days. As the time of birth approaches, the doe will become very nervous. Don't disturb her too much. If you do, she may not take care of her babies after they are born.

Four days before the young rabbits are to be born, begin feeding the doe about half the amount of food she normally eats. In this way, her body will not make too much milk, and her breasts will not become swollen and inflamed.

Before birth, the doe will pull fur from her body to

◄ Wooden nestbox.

line the nest. In winter, she may pull out almost all of her fur. Don't be alarmed; the fur will grow back.

When the time comes for the doe to "kindle," or give birth, you should leave her alone. If you try to help her, she will become upset and may kill her young.

A rabbit is born

On the day of birth, the baby rabbits lie within the uteri. For 31 days, they have been growing inside these pear-shaped structures.

Now one small head slips down into the vagina. This narrow tunnel is the baby rabbit's passageway to the outside. The doe's vagina stretches. Her uterine muscles

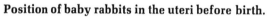

Position of baby rabbits in the uteri before birth.

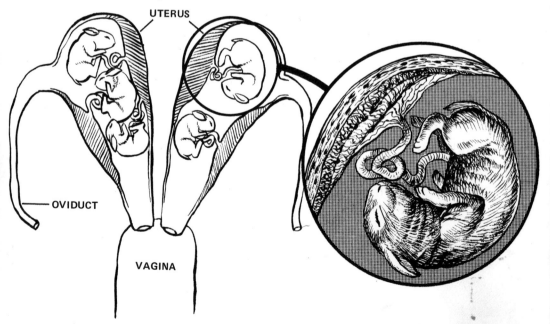

UTERUS

OVIDUCT

VAGINA

push. A baby rabbit slides slowly down the passageway and out of an opening under the doe's tail and is born.

Using her teeth, the doe pulls away the thin sac that surrounds the rabbit. This water-filled bag, called an amnion, protected the baby rabbit while it was growing inside the doe. The doe eats the sac. If it were left to decay, it would cause an odor that might attract such unfriendly animals as mice and rats.

Floating inside this bag of water, the baby rabbit could not feed or breathe for itself. Instead, all of its food and air came from the placenta, which lies inside the wall of the uterus. The placenta received food and air from the doe's blood and passed them to the baby rabbit through a long tube called an umbilical cord.

Through this same cord flowed the rabbit's wastes, which went back to the placenta. The wastes entered the doe's blood vessels and were carried away in her blood stream for the doe to pass out of her body, along with her own wastes.

When the rabbit is born, you can see one end of the cord attached to the baby rabbit's belly. The other end is connected to the placenta. The doe snips the cord with her teeth. Now the baby rabbit must breathe and feed itself.

The placenta remains attached to the uterine wall until all the baby rabbits are born. Usually, a doe has a litter of six rabbits. After the last birth, the placenta is shed and slips out through the vagina. The doe eats the placenta too. It gives her nourishment and strength, which she needs to take care of the newborn rabbits.

Caring for the family

After kindling, the doe should be left alone. She will feed the babies with her own milk, clean them, and cover them with fur from her body.

The day after birth, start giving the doe a little more food. Increase her food each day until she is eating her regular amount. When the baby rabbits are three weeks old, be sure the doe has food at all times.

You can look at the young rabbits on the third day. Attract the doe's attention with some food, or stroke her with one hand. With your other hand, examine the nest. Do not be surprised if one or two of the young rabbits are dead. They were too weak to survive. Remove any dead rabbits from the nest and bury them outside in the ground.

All the rabbits in the nest should be plump, full of milk, and lying still. If they are moving around, then the doe is probably not nursing them enough. Watch her when she goes into the nest. She should lie still in order to give her babies a chance to nurse. The doe should go into the nest box once early in the morning and once again late

Mother nursing her young. This doe had five babies, all of which lived. ▶

in the evening for about one minute each time to nurse. Her milk is so rich that the young rabbits need only a little of it to grow.

Some does refuse to nurse. If this happens, you will have to become "foster mother" to the young rabbits. Using a doll bottle and nipple, give each rabbit one bottle of warmed whole milk four times a day. Add two drops of light Karo syrup into each bottle with an eye dropper.

After the rabbits are ten days old, they can drink from a spoon. When they are big enough to lap up milk from a saucer, you can stop adding the syrup to their milk.

Baby rabbits are born almost naked and with their eyes closed. In about one week, their eyes will open and their fur will appear. If their eyes stay shut, wash them with warm water to help them open.

When the rabbits are eight weeks old, they can be

Four-day-old Dutch rabbits. Baby rabbits are born with their eyes and ears closed.

Young rabbits eating on their own as Mother watches.

weaned—not fed by their mother's milk. Separate them from the doe. You can keep the female rabbits togther, but put each male into his own hutch. Bucks kept together sometimes fight. If you want to mate these rabbits, wait until they are six months old before you breed them.

Keeping records

When raising rabbits, it is a good idea to keep a breeding record on each doe and buck. You can do **this** in a notebook. At the top of the page, write your rabbit's name. Under this, record the date on which it was mated and the name of the rabbit it was mated to. Then write down the number of offspring in each litter and the date on which they were born. Also, record their appearance, their health, and their weight.

By keeping records, you will learn which buck is the best for fathering litters and which doe produces the healthiest rabbits.

Most rabbits live five to nine years. Rather than keeping your rabbits for their entire lifetimes, you might want to give some of them away to friends so that they too can enjoy these gentle animals as pets.

Keep a breeding record.

Aside from being excellent pets, domestic rabbits are also used in scientific research. Because rabbits' bodies fight off diseases much like the human body, scientists like to use them in research projects. Rabbits react to medicines in much the same way human beings do. And their internal organs and skeleton are similar to man's. Moreover, for testing purposes, blood can easily be taken out of the large veins in their ears, and serum can be injected.

Insulin testing

Rabbits are important to the lives of several million people who have a disease called diabetes. A diabetic is a person whose body does not make proper use of sugar.

Each of us needs sugar, which we get from the food we eat, to supply energy to our bodies. In our body, a

This rabbit is being used for scientific research.

substance called insulin enables the sugar to reach muscles, fat, and other body tissues, and be "burned" to produce energy. Insulin is made by the pancreas, a gland that aids in food digestion.

For some reason, a diabetic's body is unable to make proper use of the insulin his body produces. As a result, a diabetic does not absorb enough sugar into his tissues, and his body does not have enough energy to do its work.

Diabetes cannot be cured, but it can be controlled with doses of insulin. Scientists obtain insulin from the pancreas glands of cows and pigs. After each batch of insulin is made, a sample is taken and injected into a rabbit.

Rabbits are used to test the strength of insulin because there is no chemical way to do this. Without these tests, diabetics would not know how strong each dose is. They could become very ill and, in many cases, would die.

Skin tests

Rabbits are also used to test creams and lotions, as their skin is very sensitive. A small spot on the rabbit's back is shaved and the cream or lotion is applied. Chances are that if a rabbit develops a rash or some type of allergic reaction, so will a human being who uses that same lotion or cream.

These are only two tests that show how rabbits help people. There are many more.

Whether rabbits are kept for study in research centers or in classrooms, or for the pleasure of enjoying their company at home, they make fine pets. For some of you, the discovery of the world of rabbits may well begin a lifelong interest in our natural world.

RABBIT BREEDS

Breed	Weight	Main Colors	Raised for	History
American Rabbit	8-11 lbs.	White with pink eyes, or Blue with blue eyes.	Meat, fur, show.	An American creation. First exhibited in California, 1917.
Angora (English)	5½-8 lbs.	White, black, blue, fawn.	Wool, show.	Originated in Ankara, Turkey. Its wool is silky.
Angora (French)	7-8 lbs.	White preferred.	Wool, show.	Originated in Ankara, Turkey. Appeared in France, 1723. French peasants plucked its coarse wool, spun it into strands with hand looms, and knitted the wool into garments.
Belgian Hare	8 lbs.	Chestnut with black markings. Hazel eyes surrounded by white circles.	Meat, fur, show.	Originated in Belgium. Called "the race horse" of the rabbit family because of its long body.
Beveren	9-11 lbs.	White or Blue with deep blue eyes. Black with brown eyes.	Meat, fur.	Named for the city of Beveren, Belgium.
Californian	8-10½ lbs.	White with black or gray ears, nose, feet, and tail.	Meat.	An American creation. First exhibited in California, 1928.
Champagne D'Argent	10-12 lbs.	Silver. Young are born black. In about four months, their coats turn silver.	Meat, fur.	One of the oldest domestic rabbit breeds. First mentioned in a French journal, 1730. Its name means "silver rabbit from Champagne." Champagne is the name of the French province in which this rabbit was once raised in great numbers. Argent is the French word for silver.
Checkered Giant	11-12 lbs.	Blue, black.	Meat, show.	Probably originated in Belgium. First introduced as a breed in Germany.
Chinchilla (comes in three varieties, each of which is considered a separate breed).	6½-8 lbs. 9-12 lbs. 13-16 lbs.			
Standard American Giant		Blue and white fur marked with black hairs.	Fur, show.	A French creation. First exhibited in France, 1913.

Breed	Weight	Main Colors	Raised for	History
Crème D'Argent	8-11 lbs.	Orange silver.	Meat, fur, show.	Originated in France.
Dutch	3½-5½ lbs.	Chocolate, black, gray, blue, steel-gray, tortoise.	Show.	One of the oldest breeds. Ancestor was the Brabanco rabbit, which was named for the Dutch province of Brabant. Called the Panda rabbit because of its markings.
English Spot	5-8 lbs.	Black, blue, tortoise, gold, lilac, gray, chocolate.	Meat, show.	One of the oldest show or fancy breeds. First exhibited in England, 1885. Called the English butterfly rabbit because of the butterfly mark on its nose.
Flemish Giant	12-15 lbs.	Gray, black, sandy, white, fawn, blue.	Meat, fur.	Origin unknown. Thought to come from Flanders.
Florida White	4-6 lbs.	All white.	Meat, laboratory.	Ancestors are the Dutch, Polish, and New Zealand white rabbits.
Harlequin (once called Japanese)	6-8 lbs.	Black, blue, chocolate, and lilac. These colors alternate with orange or white.	Show.	A French creation. First exhibited in Paris, France, 1887. Fur shows a spectacular color pattern.
Havana	6-7 lbs.	Chocolate, blue.	Meat, fur, show.	Originated in the Netherlands, about 1898. Named Havana because the chocolate variety's color may have been associated with the color of Havana cigars.
Himalayan	3½-5 lbs.	White with black nose, ears, feet, and tail. Young are born white, tinged with gray.	Fur, show.	One of the oldest breeds. Originated in the Himalayan Mountain area of Asia.
Lilac	6-9 lbs.	Light lilac.	Meat, fur, show.	First exhibited in England, 1913.
Lops	9-11 lbs.	Solid and broken colors.	Show.	One of the oldest breeds. First appeared in Algiers, North Africa. Drooping ears are about two feet long from tip to tip. Record length is 28½ inches.
Netherland Dwarf	2-2½ lbs.	Greatest variety of colors and coat patterns of all the breeds.	Show.	Smallest of all the breeds. First appeared in the Netherlands.

Breed	Weight	Main Colors	Raised for	History
New Zealand	10-12 lbs.	White, red, black.	Meat, fur, show, laboratory.	An American creation. First appeared in the United States, 1900s.
Palomino	9-11 lbs.	Gold, lynx.	Meat.	An American creation.
Polish	2½-3½ lbs.	White with blue or ruby eyes. Black, chocolate.	Fur, show.	Origin unknown. First appeared in England, 1884. This is the rabbit magicians pull out of the hat. Used in early American vaudeville shows. Nicknamed the "Little Aristocrat."
Rex	8-9 lbs.	Black, blue, chocolate.	Meat, fur, show.	A French creation, 1919.
Sable (includes the the Siamese Sable breed)	5-9 lbs.	Brown. Siamese breed's color resembles the coat of a Siamese cat.	Show.	Result of many Chinchilla matings.
Satin	9-11 lbs.	Nine colors, including red, blue, Siamese.	Meat, fur, show.	First appeared in the United States, 1931.
Silver	4-7 lbs.	Gray, fawn, brown.	Show.	Existed thousands of years ago in India and brought to Europe by Portuguese sailors early in the seventeenth century.
Silver Fox	8-12 lbs.	Black and dark blue.	Meat, fur.	An American creation. This rabbit's long, silvery fur resembles fox fur.
Silver Marten	6½-9½ lbs.	Black, blue, chocolate, sable.	Fur, show.	Unknown origin. Known in England as the Silver Fox rabbit.
Tan	4-6 lbs.	Black, blue, chocolate, lilac.	Show.	First produced in England, 1880s.

Index